GLA

A MISCELLANY

Compiled by Julia Skinner

With particular reference to the work of
Clive Hardy, Bill Bissett and Dr James Mackay

THE FRANCIS FRITH COLLECTION

www.francisfrith.com

First published in the United Kingdom in 2006 by The Francis Frith Collection®

This edition published in 2014
ISBN 978-1-84589-776-5
Text and Design copyright The Francis Frith Collection®
Photographs copyright The Francis Frith Collection® except where indicated.

The Frith® photographs and the Frith® logo are reproduced under licence from
Heritage Photographic Resources Ltd, the owners of the Frith® archive and trademarks.
'The Francis Frith Collection', 'Francis Frith' and 'Frith' are registered trademarks of
Heritage Photographic Resources Ltd.

All rights reserved. No photograph in this publication may be sold to a third party other than in the original
form of this publication, or framed for sale to a third party. No parts of this publication may be reproduced,
stored in a retrieval system, or transmitted, in any form, or by any means, electronic, mechanical, photocopying,
recording or otherwise, without the prior permission of the publishers and copyright holder.

British Library Cataloguing in Publication Data

Did You Know? Glasgow - A Miscellany
Compiled by Julia Skinner
With particular reference to the work of Clive Hardy, Bill Bissett and Dr James Mackay

The Francis Frith Collection
6 Oakley Business Park,
Wylye Road, Dinton,
Wiltshire SP3 5EU
Tel: +44 (0) 1722 716 376
Email: info@francisfrith.co.uk
www.francisfrith.com

Printed and bound in England

Front Cover: **GLASGOW, THE BROOMIELAW 1897** 39799p

The colour-tinting is for illustrative purposes only, and is not intended to be historically accurate

AS WITH ANY HISTORICAL DATABASE, THE FRANCIS FRITH ARCHIVE IS CONSTANTLY BEING
CORRECTED AND IMPROVED, AND THE PUBLISHERS WOULD WELCOME INFORMATION ON
OMISSIONS OR INACCURACIES

CONTENTS

- 2 Introduction
- 4 Local Names and Phrases
- 5 Haunted Glasgow
- 6 Glasgow Miscellany
- 44 Sporting Glasgow
- 46 Quiz Questions
- 48 Recipes
- 52 Quiz Answers
- 54 Francis Frith - Pioneer Victorian Photographer

Did You Know?
GLASGOW
A MISCELLANY

INTRODUCTION

In the 18th century the advent of overseas trade established Glasgow's potential as a port and industrial centre, trading with the American colonies in particular. An especially important import was tobacco - Glasgow's tobacco merchants were known as the Tobacco Lords. American requirements for textiles transformed Scotland's linen industry to such an extent that by 1778 there were 4,000 handlooms in Glasgow alone. After the American War of Independence, the price of flax rocketed and cotton was looked upon as a viable alternative. By 1787, no fewer than nineteen cotton mills were at work in the city, rising to over 200 within a few decades. Sugar was almost as important to the city's economy, and the first sugar refinery was opened in Glasgow as early as 1675. By the mid 18th century Glasgow was the leading centre for the production of sugar, molasses and rum.

The geographical advantage of Glasgow's position, straddling the River Clyde, meant that the Industrial Revolution in the following century resulted in a huge expansion of heavy engineering, steel and ironworks. It was the advent of steam power that saw the development of the two greatest industries in the Glasgow and Clydebank area - shipbuilding and the manufacture of railway locomotives. The shipyards included John Brown & Co of Clydebank, A & J Inglis Ltd and D & W Henderson & Co. In 1840 the Clyde shipyards were turning out about 250 tons of shipping each year; by 1865 this had risen to about 125,000 tons a year, and the amount doubled a decade later, but by 1908 it peaked at 757,000 tons per annum. The Clyde yards were extremely versatile, building every conceivable type of vessel, from luxury yachts to canal barges, from gunboats to battleships, from lake steamers to river dredges. By the 1890s a third of all ships launched in the UK came from the Clyde. Glasgow's shipyards were at that time building battleships, cruisers

Did You Know?
GLASGOW
A MISCELLANY

and other warships for half the world's navies, as well as constructing the fastest, largest and most luxurious liners for the great shipping companies. Railway locomotives were manufactured by the North British Locomotive Co, an amalgamation of three companies employing 7,000 workers. In total the NBL built about 20,000 railway locomotives for customers world-wide.

Glasgow also became famous for its many public parks, theatres and music halls, and by the latter half of the 19th century Glasgow could proudly claim to have become 'the second city of the Empire'.

The din of the jackhammers and riveters of the area's shipbuilding industry died down in the 1960s, and today only one shipyard is still in existence, Kvaerner Govan, owned by a Norwegian company. Even the amount of shipping on the Clyde dropped dramatically in the 1970s with the advent of air freight. For more than a decade the Clyde has been silent, the docks and wharves falling into decay. However, even as the heavy industries of Clydeside vanished, Glasgow was diversifying into new areas of employment, reflected in the development of high-tech industries, information technology and call-centres, and has become an important conference centre. This has resulted in an astonishing transformation of the city, particularly along the waterfront. Glasgow is moving into the 21st century as a forward-looking city that is developing into a major world centre for sport, culture and tourism.

Did You Know?
GLASGOW
A MISCELLANY

LOCAL NAMES AND PHRASES

The Glasgow football clubs of Rangers and Celtic are popularly known as **'the Old Firm'**.

The first craft guild in Glasgow was that of the skinners in 1516, followed by the tailors (1527), weavers (1528) and hammermen (1536). By the end of the 16th century other guilds had been formed, but there was a long-running dispute over the number which came under the control of the Deacon Convenor. It was from this dispute that the common expression **'at sixes and sevens'** came about, implying a state of chaos and disorder.

The first monument anywhere in the British Empire to the memory of Admiral Lord Nelson was erected by public subscription on Glasgow Green within months of his death at the Battle of Trafalgar in October 1805. **'To face the monument'** was a Glasgow euphemism for a public hanging, because public executions took place near the Nelson monument on Glasgow Green, outside the South Prison. The last public execution in Glasgow took place in 1865, when Dr Edward Pritchard was hanged for poisoning his wife and mother-in-law.

'Glasgow made the Clyde, and the Clyde made Glasgow' was a popular local saying in the heyday of the shipbuilding industry.

HAUNTED GLASGOW

There have been many reported sightings of a ghostly woman at the Shields Road Underground Station. The woman is believed to have committed suicide by throwing herself under a train as it was pulling into the station, and her ghost has been seen on the platform and also on the railway track. Another haunted underground station in Glasgow is Hillhead, where sightings of the ghost of a lady in evening dress have been reported by staff at the station. The mysterious lady appears to walk along the platform and is said to sing happily before disappearing into one of the underground tunnels.

The 19th century Cathedral House Hotel in Cathedral Square is said to have several resident spectres. One is supposed to haunt the staircase, and two ghostly children are said to roam the top floor of the hotel.

The Tron Theatre has been the scene of many mysterious occurrences, including sightings of people in old-fashioned clothes looking out from the tower, and what staff described as a strange and threatening presence in the shape of a 'dark figure' in the boiler room. A variety of other strange apparitions are said to roam the auditorium after performances as well as the bar and box office, where the sighting of a man dressed in riding gear has been reported. The theatre has been the scene of several paranormal investigations, the most recent being in February 2006, when it was investigated by The Ghost Club. Derek Green's report can be read on www.ghostclub.org.uk/tron.htm

The Theatre Royal is supposed to be haunted by the ghost of a former cleaner called Nora. She had hopes of becoming an actress, but when she realised that her dream would never come true she threw herself to her death from the upper circle of the theatre, and now haunts the building by slamming doors.

The Glasgow Royal Infirmary in Castle Street is associated with two ghostly ladies. A 'Green Lady' in the surgical block is supposed to be the ghost of a nun who died after falling down a stairwell, and a 'Grey Lady' is said to glide silently along corridors in the building.

Did You Know?
GLASGOW
A MISCELLANY

GLASGOW MISCELLANY

An elaborate statue of Glasgow's patron saint, St Mungo, can be seen at the north entrance of the Kelvingrove Museum; the saint's real name was Kentigern, but he was given the nickname of Mungo ('my dear one') by St Serf, who cared for him as a child, and it is as St Mungo that he is best-known in Glasgow. St Mungo chose Glasgow as the site for his church in the second half of the sixth century, and his portrait and miraculous symbols adorn the civic arms.

By the time of St Mungo's death in AD612, Glasgow may have been little more than a line of mud huts straggling southwards from the church on the site where the cathedral now stands. From Townhead you can look down the length of the High Street to the Tolbooth and the Mercat Cross, around which the medieval market town developed.

Glasgow received its first charter from King William the Lion c1175, and for the first time it was designated by the Latin term 'civitas' (city). A few years later the king granted Bishop Jocelin the right to hold an annual fair, a tradition that continues to this day, although by 1830 it had been transformed into a great festival for the working people of the city. The medieval fair was held at the upper end of the High Street (Townhead), but as Glasgow began to spread southward the fair moved to the north bank of the Clyde, near the Stockwell. After it ceased to be primarily a market for horses and cattle in 1818 it moved to the western end of what is now Glasgow Green, and was given over to a circus, menagerie and sideshows.

RENFIELD STREET 1897 39769a

Did You Know?
GLASGOW
A MISCELLANY

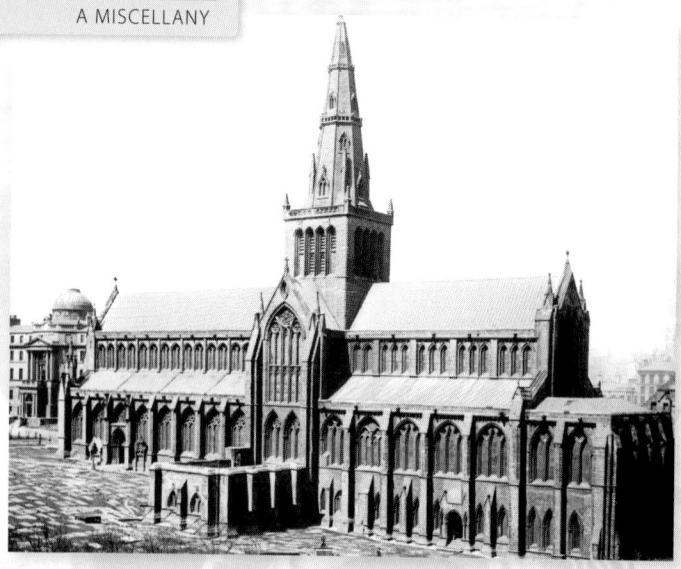

Did You Know?
GLASGOW
A MISCELLANY

THE CATHEDRAL 1897 39775

The see of Glasgow was put on a proper footing in 1125, with the erection of the first cathedral on the site of St Mungo's original church. That structure burned down in 1175, but the cathedral was rebuilt between 1180 and 1195 and again between 1250 and 1300, resulting in the fine Gothic structure that stands to this day (see photograph 39775, above). The cathedral has gone through many periods of peace and strife, and on one door of the building lead shot can still be seen, which bears witness to the Glasgow citizens' successful defence of the cathedral against the Reformation zealots of the 16th century who would have destroyed it.

Did You Know?
GLASGOW
A MISCELLANY

Glasgow Cathedral survives almost intact from medieval times and is said to be the most complete in Scotland, having lost only its western towers, which were dismantled in the 19th century.

Below the choir of the cathedral is the crypt, part of which dates from the 1190s. It is well proportioned with fine pillars and vaulting (see photograph 39783, below). In the centre of the crypt is the site of the tomb of St Mungo, and it was over his grave that the first church was erected in the 6th century.

THE CATHEDRAL CRYPT 1897 39783

Did You Know?
GLASGOW
A MISCELLANY

Did You Know?
GLASGOW
A MISCELLANY

BUCHANAN STREET 1897 39767

Buchanan Street, seen in this photograph, was one of the busiest thoroughfares in 19th-century Glasgow. At one end was the Caledonian Railway Station, where trains could be caught for Oban, Perth and the north; at the other was the St Enoch Station. St Enoch Station was gutted in 1977 to make way for the St Enoch Centre, constructed in 1981-89, a vast shopping complex which looks more like a railway station than the building it replaced.

THE CATHEDRAL, THE CHOIR EAST 1897 39780

The choir of the cathedral dates from the 13th century, and contains a superb 15th-century stone screen. Behind the choir are the Chapter House, which has a richly carved doorway, and the Lady Chapel. In the Chapter House is a memorial to the memory of the nine martyred Covenanters, who were executed for their Presbyterian beliefs during the religious conflict of the 17th century known as 'the Killing Time'.

> The Gorbals developed south of the river beyond the Brig Port. The area was originally a leper colony, and later became a congested slum whose lawlessness was proverbial.

Did You Know?
GLASGOW
A MISCELLANY

Between 1861 and 1881 Glasgow experienced four major cholera outbreaks. Rickets and tuberculosis were endemic amongst the city's mill workers, and smallpox was rife. During this period, a quarter of all children born to mill workers died before reaching their first birthday.

The nave of the cathedral with its timbered ceiling was completed in 1480. At a later date it was divided into three congregations, the nave, choir and crypt. In photograph 39778, below, we can see the screen separating the nave and choir. During the 19th century the windows throughout the cathedral were filled with stained-glass, most of it from Munich, at a cost close to £100,000.

THE CATHEDRAL, THE NAVE EAST 1897 39778

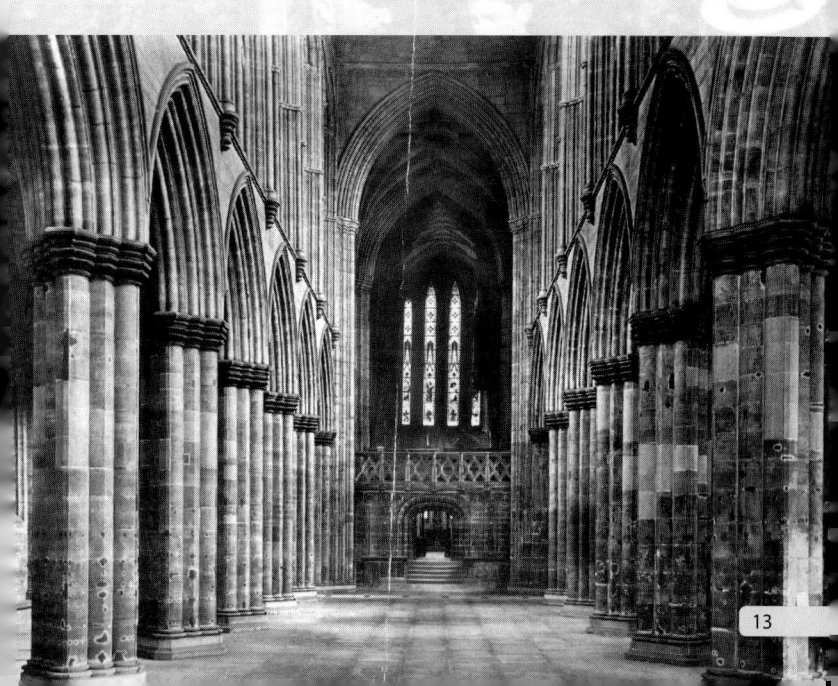

Did You Know?
GLASGOW
A MISCELLANY

In 1302 William 'Braveheart' Wallace, conducting a guerrilla war against the English occupying forces, attacked the Bishop's Castle (formerly next to the cathedral) which was defended by Anthony Beck, Bishop of Durham. The English troops repelled the Scots, and there then ensued a running battle down the High Street. The day was saved by Wallace's uncle, Auchinleck, who counter-attacked with 140 men concealed in the Drygate and put the enemy garrison to flight.

Glasgow University was founded by Bishop William Turnbull in 1451. The Papal Bull establishing the university cited the advantages of Glasgow's location: 'the air is mild, victuals are plentiful, and great store of other things pertaining to the use of man is found'. Classes were originally conducted in the cathedral crypt, but then moved to a building in the High Street. Over the centuries this developed into a splendid structure with twin quadrangles. With the phenomenal commercial and industrial expansion of Glasgow in the 19th century this site became too cramped, so in 1870 the university sold the land for a railway goods yard - hence College Goods Station, now demolished to make way for luxury flats. A new university building designed by Sir George Gilbert Scott, seen in photograph 39787, opposite, was built, perched on Gilmorehill above the River Kelvin. The main building consists of two quadrangles surmounted by the tower and spire completed by the architect's son, J Oldrid Scott, between 1887 and 1891.

Did You Know?
GLASGOW
A MISCELLANY

GLASGOW UNIVERSITY 1897 39787

Did You Know?
GLASGOW
A MISCELLANY

THE BROOMIELAW 1897 39800

Glasgow was never a walled town, but it had four gates at the points of the compass, to control traffic. These gates were known as ports and were called the Stable Green Port (north), the Gallowgate Port (east), Brig Port (south) and Trongate Port (west). Rather confusingly, the streets were called gates (often spelled 'gait' or 'yet'). East and west of the Cross were the Trongate and Gallowgate, still the principal thoroughfares leading to Argyle Street and the Edinburgh Road respectively. The Briggate, or Bridgegate, linked the north end of the bridge to the Saltmarket (originally called the Waulcergait, meaning 'the street of the wool-scourers'), while the Drygate ran east from the cathedral and terminated on the west bank of the Molendinar.

Did You Know?
GLASGOW
A MISCELLANY

The growth of medieval Glasgow was hampered by the rivalry of its larger and more powerful neighbours, Dumbarton, Renfrew and Rutherglen, which were royal burghs from the early 12th century and often tried to exact tolls and taxes on goods going to or from Glasgow. When Glasgow was finally raised to the dignity of a royal burgh in its own right in the early 17th century the following craftsmen were registered within its boundaries: 65 tailors, 55 maltsters, 50 cordiners (shoe-makers), 30 weavers, 27 hammermen, 27 bakers, 23 coopers, 21 skinners, 21 wrights, 17 fleshers, 11 masons, 7 bonnet-makers, 5 dyers and 2 surgeons.

THE CATHEDRAL 1897 39772

Did You Know?
GLASGOW
A MISCELLANY

Argyle Street was originally a rather unpleasant street, known officially as Westergait but commonly referred to as the Shitt Wynd. It was drained, sanitised and renamed Anderston Walk, but in 1751 its name was changed again, to Argyll Street in honour of John Campbell, the 2nd Duke of Argyll (1678-1743), the most

Did You Know?
GLASGOW
A MISCELLANY

ardent champion of the Act of Union (1707) and commander of the Hanoverian troops who defeated the Jacobites in the rebellion of 1715. The spelling 'Argyle' was adopted by 1826, although the form 'Argyll' was reverted to for a brief period in the 1880s.

ARGYLE STREET 1897 39765

Did You Know?
GLASGOW
A MISCELLANY

THE MUNICIPAL BUILDINGS 1897 39760

THE ROYAL EXCHANGE 1897 39798

Did You Know?
GLASGOW
A MISCELLANY

The first bridge over the Clyde was a wooden structure erected in 1245. It was replaced c1410 by a more substantial stone bridge with eight arches. For centuries this bridge was the only one linking Glasgow to the Gorbals, Govan and Rutherglen. By the middle of the 18th century it was in dire need of repair, and Glasgow was compelled to undertake expensive reconstruction in 1776. Thomas Telford, the father of civil engineering, supervised its widening in 1821. It was dismantled in 1847 and eventually replaced by the Victoria Bridge, which opened in 1854.

> By the mid 18th century the Glasgow Bridge was proving to be a bottleneck to cross-river traffic. In 1767 construction of a second bridge, at the Broomielaw, commenced under John Smeaton, the famous lighthouse builder. It was completed in 1772 and named the Jamaica Bridge, after the street that ran north from it and, in turn, reflected the importance of the sugar plantations of the West Indies to the city's growth. Half a century later this bridge was inadequate to deal with the volume of traffic, and in 1836 it was replaced by a bridge designed by Thomas Telford. This gave way to the third and present Jamaica Bridge in 1899, although the decorative features of the Telford Bridge were retained.

One day in 1765 young James Watt, an instrument maker to the university, was crossing Glasgow Green when the idea of a separate condenser for the steam engine occurred to him. He had been given a Newcomen engine to tinker with, but it was so inefficient as to be useless. Watt put his idea into practice, and converted what had been almost a toy into a machine which rapidly replaced wind and water power. It is no exaggeration to say that the Industrial Revolution was born on Glasgow Green, and an engraved boulder marks the spot.

Did You Know?
GLASGOW
A MISCELLANY

Photograph 39769, opposite, shows a convoy of horse-drawn trams trundling along Renfield Street in 1897. Within a year electric street trams would be running, and the horse-drawn trams beginning to be phased out. Glasgow was the last city in the UK to abandon its tramway system, in 1962, and the anchoring hooks for the tramway overhead wires are still evident on many buildings throughout the city. Examples of the tramcars can be seen at the Transport Museum in the Kelvin Hall.

The conversion of Glasgow's textile mills to steam power and the advent of power looms created an enormous cotton industry, and by 1830 about a third of the city's workforce was employed in this sector alone. This phenomenal expansion had its downside, particularly affecting the handloom weavers who had earned high wages before the advent of the power looms. Men who had worked in their own homes were now supplanted by vast armies of girls working in the mills. Industrial unrest, unemployment in the aftermath of the Napoleonic Wars and wage cuts culminated in the Radical Risings of 1820. Trouble began in 1819 in the Calton district and spread to other parts of the city. The uprising in April 1820 was a feeble affair and appears to have been fomented by an agent provocateur, but 22 weavers were apprehended by the military at Bonnymuir. 19 of them were convicted and transported to Botany Bay, but the ringleaders were hanged and beheaded. In 1847 their remains were reburied at the highest point of Sighthill Cemetery, and the Martyrs' Memorial was erected. One of these men was Andrew Hardie, great-grandfather of James Keir Hardie, the founder in 1893 of the Independent Labour Party.

Did You Know?
GLASGOW
A MISCELLANY

RENFIELD STREET 1897 39769

THE VIEW ON THE KELVIN 1897 39758

GEORGE SQUARE 1897 39759

Glasgow's George Square has been said to remind visiting Londoners of Trafalgar Square, but the central column is a monument to the author Sir Walter Scott rather than Lord Nelson (see photograph 39759, above). The square served to emphasise Glasgow's self-proclaimed status as 'the second city of the Empire'. The magnificent municipal buildings around George Square were completed in 1888, including the Post Office, the Bank of Scotland, the Merchants' House (the large building in the centre background, opened in 1877) and several hotels. There are many statues of other famous Victorian figures in the square, including the only equestrian statue of Queen Victoria ever made. Her husband Prince Albert, also on horseback, is nearby.

In 1822 Richard Campbell was the last man to be publicly flogged through the streets of Glasgow by the public hangman. His crime had been to lead a mob in an attack on the house of John Provand, who was suspected of being a body-snatcher who dug up recently buried bodies to sell to the anatomy schools for dissection practice.

Photograph 39768, below, shows the Grand Hotel, with Charing Cross Mansions in the background. The Mansions still exist, but the Grand Hotel was demolished to make way for the M8 motorway, Kingston Bridge crossing over the Clyde at this point.

THE GRAND HOTEL, CHARING CROSS 1897 39768

Did You Know?
GLASGOW
A MISCELLANY

Behind the cathedral is the Necropolis (see photograph 39784, below), which contains a number of substantial monuments to the great and the good of Glasgow, as well as to those who had enough money to make sure that when they were gone

THE NECROPOLIS 1897 39784

Did You Know?
GLASGOW
A MISCELLANY

they would not be forgotten. The large statue on the pedestal at the highest point of the Necropolis was erected in 1825 to the memory of the reformer John Knox - this was the first statue of Knox to be erected in Scotland.

Did You Know?
GLASGOW
A MISCELLANY

THE WESTERN INFIRMARY 1897 39788

THE ROYAL INFIRMARY 1897 39789

28

The Boys' Brigade was founded in Glasgow in 1883, by William Smith at the Woodside Mission Hall of the Free Church. The movement spread rapidly throughout the UK, and to every part of the world where there were Scottish churches. The guest of honour at the Boys' Brigade rally of 1903 was Major-General Baden-Powell, who was so impressed by the discipline of the boys that he organised the Scouting Movement. Following the experimental camp at Brownsea Island, Dorset, in 1907, boys from four local schools (Glasgow and Kelvinside Academies, and Hillhead and Glasgow High Schools) joined in September that year in Athole Gardens, Hillhead, to form the world's first official Scout troop - now the First Glasgow Scout Group.

Photograph 39789, opposite, shows the old Royal Infirmary, which was designed by Robert and James Adam and opened in 1794. The infirmary was extended several times during the 19th century, and was demolished and rebuilt in the early 20th century. It was here in 1865 that Lord Joseph Lister pioneered antiseptic surgery whilst a professor at Glasgow University, and first began antiseptic treatment; his original carbolic spray is now one of the exhibits in the university's Hunterian Museum. The Royal Infirmary was also where Dr John Macintyre was the first person to use X-rays for diagnosis. The infirmary was sited next door to the cathedral, and was just a hearse's ride away from the Necropolis. At the end of the 19th century, 430,000 people were crammed into central Glasgow and the city's tenement blocks were a breeding ground for all manner of contagious diseases.

The Botanic Gardens occupy 43 acres off Great Western Road. Many rare orchids, tree ferns and tropical plants are grown here, including bananas. The Botanic Gardens were originally primarily for the benefit of members of the Royal Botanic Institution of Glasgow who established the first gardens near Sauchiehall Street. The Kibble Palace was originally the conservatory of a mansion on the shore of Loch Long and was offered to Glasgow's Botanic Society; it was erected in the Botanic Gardens in 1873 and is the largest glasshouse in the UK. It is now a Winter Garden, but was formerly used for public meetings and concerts. The Kibble Palace was dismantled in 2004 to allow it to be repaired and expanded, and it is hoped that in its restored and re-erected state it will once again be used for public functions.

The central feature of photograph 39794, opposite, taken in 1897, is the Stewart memorial fountain in Kelvingrove Park which commemorates Robert Stewart, the Glasgow Lord Provost who inaugurated the city's supply of clean water from Loch Katrine. Sir Joseph Paxton, the designer of the Crystal Palace in London, laid out this park on the banks of the River Kelvin, and it was opened in 1853. The Art Gallery and Museum in the grounds is the largest civic museum and art gallery in the UK, and has recently reopened after a major refurbishment.

> Arguably Glasgow's oldest and best-known statue is that of William III on horseback, which was presented to the city by James Macrae, Governor of Madras, in 1735, in memory of the tercentenary of the Glorious Revolution which put the Protestant King William on the throne in place of the Catholic James II. The statue has moved around Glasgow several times, having been shifted from the Cross to the middle of the Trongate in 1898, and then to Cathedral Square Gardens in 1926. Allegedly the horse's tail was fitted with a ball and socket joint to allow it to move in the wind.

Did You Know?
GLASGOW
A MISCELLANY

THE BOTANIC GARDENS 39796

KELVINGROVE PARK 1897 39794

A great hindrance to the expansion of Glasgow's trade to Scandinavia and north-western Europe had been the hazardous voyage round the western and northern coast of Scotland. As early as 1726, Daniel Defoe had suggested the tremendous advantage of 'a Navigation from the Forth to the Clyde'. John Smeaton carried out a feasibility study in 1762, and an Act of Parliament was passed in 1768 to allow the construction of a canal. Work began at the eastern end and got as far as Hamiltonhill on the outskirts of Glasgow by 1777. The American War and the resulting economic downturn brought work to a halt for lack of funds. After the Jacobite Rebellion of 1745, money from forfeited Jacobite estates was pumped into the project in 1784, and it was completed six years later. In 1795 the canalisation of the upper Clyde was undertaken: the channel was dredged and deepened, and the riverbanks were lined with masonry. Within a decade it was widened and deepened again, permitting ocean-going vessels to come all the way up-river to the Broomielaw. In 1810 only four foreign ships, averaging less than 10 tons each, reached the Broomielaw. In the same year the number of vessels registered at Glasgow was 24, with a total tonnage of 1,956. Five years later Glasgow was declared a head port; with the advent of steam it soon eclipsed Port Glasgow on the lower Clyde, which had been developed in the 1660s. For more than a century ships had transferred their cargoes there into small vessels called gabbarts, which could negotiate the shallows of the river and unload at the Broomielaw. While Glasgow now became its own port, Port Glasgow developed into a manufacturing town.

As early as 1788, William Symington harnessed a steam engine to paddlewheels, and the world's first steamboat took to the waters of Dalswinton Loch. In 1802 at Grangemouth, Symington perfected the 'Charlotte Dundas', which was designed as a tug-boat on the Forth and Clyde Canal (opened in 1790); however, the operators of the horse-drawn barges argued that the wash from the tug's paddles would erode the canal banks. A decade later, Henry Bell launched his 30-ton 'Comet' on the Clyde and operated a regular passenger and freight service between Glasgow and Greenock.

Did You Know?
GLASGOW
A MISCELLANY

THE BROOMIELAW 1897 39799

Did You Know?
GLASGOW
A MISCELLANY

Photograph 39801, below, was taken looking along the Broomielaw towards Clyde Street. This view shows the railway bridge serving Central Station, whilst immediately behind it work is underway on rebuilding Glasgow Bridge. It is also possible

THE BROOMIELAW 1897 39801

Did You Know?
GLASGOW
A MISCELLANY

to make out the towers of the suspension bridge situated a little further along the river. On the far bank are some of the warehouses along Bridge Wharf.

Did You Know?
GLASGOW
A MISCELLANY

The upper Clyde was not just famous as a shipbuilding area, it also developed into one of the largest ports in Europe. By the 1860s the number of ships at anchor in the upper Clyde was so great that as many as six ships would tie up alongside each other. The problem of congestion in the river was solved by the creation of three great docks or tidal basins, Kingston Dock, Queen's Dock and Prince's Dock. Farther downsteam was the series of three great graving docks at Govan, constructed between 1869 and 1898. With the decline of Clyde shipping after the Second World War these facilities became obsolete. The Kingston Dock was filled in during the early 1960s to form the southern base of the Kingston Bridge, while Queen's Dock is now the site of the Scottish Exhibition and Convention Centre. Prince's Dock provided the site for the Garden Festival in 1988. The Govan graving docks closed in 1988 and are now derelict, awaiting redevelopment; the building shown in photograph G11706, opposite, on the outer graving dock at Govan dates from the 1890s, and reflects the Italianate influence on Glasgow's architecture at the end of the 19th century.

The Drygate was the scene of an IRA gun battle in April 1921 when 30 gunmen attempted to free Frank McCarty, a leading IRA figure who was being driven from the High Court back to Duke Street Prison. Inspector Robert Johnston was killed and Detective Sergeant Stirton was wounded, but the plot failed and the gunmen were driven off. The bullet holes on the wall of the prison became a grim tourist attraction, and although Duke Street Prison was demolished in 1955 the high buttressed wall remains, and the bullet holes can still be seen to this day.

Did You Know?
GLASGOW
A MISCELLANY

**A DERELICT BUILDING AT THE
GOVAN GRAVING DOCK 2005** G11706

Did You Know?
GLASGOW
A MISCELLANY

CLYDEBANK, GLASGOW ROAD c1900 C208005

CLYDEBANK, KILBOWIE ROAD 1900 C208002

Did You Know?
GLASGOW
A MISCELLANY

In 1872 a shipyard which had moved from Govan in Glasgow became established at what is now Clydebank, and its first ship was launched in the same year. Clydebank soon developed into a large working township. The shipbuilding company of John Brown, which moved here from Sheffield when it took over James and George Thomson's shipyard in 1899, built many famous liners. These included the 'Lusitania' (1906), the 'Queen Mary', (1934), the 'Queen Elizabeth', (1938), and the 'Queen Elizabeth II' (1967).

In 1884 the Singer Manufacturing Company from America set up a sewing-machine factory in Clydebank, and the Singer's clock tower was a local landmark for many years until it was demolished in 1963.

Photograph C208002, opposite, shows Kilbowie Road in Clydebank in 1900. In 1890 only the building on the left of the photograph existed - it was built by Singer to house their workers. By 1900 the tenements have appeared along what was formerly a tree-lined road. The congested canal bridge in this photograph was replaced by a metal swingbridge in 1916, after very heated and protracted meetings between Glasgow Corporation and Clydebank Burgh regarding responsibility for the cost.

In March 1941, during the Second World War, Clydebank was almost totally destroyed by enemy bombing, suffering the heaviest bombing in the UK. Only seven houses in the burgh were undamaged, over 4,300 were destroyed or damaged beyond repair, and many people were killed. The main target was John Brown & Co's shipyard, but this was able to continue production despite the air raids.

Did You Know?
GLASGOW
A MISCELLANY

Hundreds of men from 'Red Clydeside' fought in the International Brigades during the Spanish Civil War of the 1930s. The Glasgow connection with the men who fought fascism in Spain is recalled in the statue of the Republican activist Dolores Ibarruri, popularly known as 'La Pasionara', which was erected in 1980 on Glasgow's Custom House Quay. Dolores Ibarruri was famous for declaring 'It is better to be the widows of heroes than the wives of cowards!'.

> Crookston Castle, shown in photograph 39808, opposite, was where Mary, Queen of Scots and Henry, Lord Darnley came following their marriage in July 1565. The castle was owned by Henry's father, the Earl of Lennox. The estate was held in the 12th century by Sir Robert Croc of Neilston, and it is from him that the castle derives its name. The tower was probably built in the early 15th century by Sir John Stewart, Constable of the Scots in the French service. This was the first property to be acquired by the National Trust for Scotland, in 1931.

Charles Rennie Mackintosh, born in 1868, was a Glasgow architect whose reputation is worldwide. He evolved the Glasgow Style at the turn of the 19th and 20th centuries, a middle point between Art Nouveau and Art Deco, and designed the Glasgow School of Art, the Scotland Street School (now the Museum of Education) and Miss Cranston's Willow Tea Rooms at 217 Sauchiehall Street. He was one of the first architects and interior designers to devise everything for his buildings, down to wall hangings and cutlery. His design for 'The House of an Art Lover', which won a German design competition in 1906, was realised in the 1990s and stands in Bellahouston Park.

Did You Know?
GLASGOW
A MISCELLANY

CROOKSTON CASTLE 1897 39808

THE UNIVERSITY AND THE BANDSTAND 1897 39785

Did You Know?
GLASGOW
A MISCELLANY

SAUCHIEHALL STREET 1897 39763

The section of Sauchiehall Street seen in photograph 39763, above, is now pedestrianised. Most of the buildings shown in this view have now gone, and there is a large indoor shopping complex and car parking facilities where the clock tower once stood. This is Glasgow's most famous street, renowned as a shopping venue lined with quality stores, but its name betrays its rural origins: 'saugh' is the Scots word for a willow tree and 'haugh' (later corrupted to 'hall') is the word for a meadow.

Did You Know?
GLASGOW
A MISCELLANY

'The Green Man' is the nickname for the green-patinated bronze statue of Donald Dewar which stands at the top of Buchanan Street, in front of the Royal Concert Hall. Born and educated in Glasgow, he became Scottish Secretary in 1995 and Scotland's first minister in 2000. The statue originally showed Dewar wearing spectacles but they were removed by a souvenir hunter.

The incorporation of salmon in the Glasgow coat of arms reflects the enormous importance to the city of the River Clyde in former times for the bounty of its fish. So plentiful was salmon in the 17th century that servants in the city stipulated that they should not be forced to eat it more than twice a week! No salmon could have survived in the industrially-polluted river of the 19th and early 20th centuries, but in the post-industrial city of the 21st century salmon - and many other species of fish - are once more in the Clyde.

WOODSIDE PLACE 1897 39762

SPORTING GLASGOW

Queen's Park Football Club, founded in 1867, is not only Scotland's oldest football club but the only League club to remain wholly amateur. The club instigated the first ever football international, on St Andrew's Day 1872, between Scotland and England. The club's ground at Hampden Park is also the venue for Scotland's international football matches. It has recently been refurbished and can seat 52,000. Notable players for Queen's Park FC include Andrew Watson (the first black player to play for Scotland), Sir Alex Ferguson (manager of Manchester United), and R S McColl, who scored a hat-trick at the 1909 Scotland-England international; he was popularly known as 'Toffee Bob' because of the chain of confectionery shops all over Glasgow that he founded with his brother Tom.

'The Old Firm Game' between Rangers and Celtic at Ibrox Park in 1939 was watched by 119,000 spectators, the largest attendance at a League football match anywhere in the UK.

Benny Lynch, born in the Gorbals in 1913, won the world flyweight championship in 1935, the first Scot to win a major international boxing title. He won 82 of his 110 bouts and retained his title until 1938, when he was over the weight limit for the match with the American Jacky Jurich.

Rangers FC has had only twelve managers in its history. The first was William Wilton, who was appointed in 1899, and led the club to seven League titles before being tragically drowned in a boating accident. After Wilton, the club had just two more managers prior to 1967, Bill Struth from 1920-1954 and Scot Symon from 1954-1967. Struth's 34-year reign is surely unique - during this period Rangers won eighteen Scottish championships, including five in succession from 1927-1931.

Did You Know?
GLASGOW
A MISCELLANY

Celtic Football Club holds two important attendance records. The 1938 Scottish Cup final win against Aberdeen attracted 146,433 spectators, a record for a club match in Europe. The attendance of 133,961 for the European Cup semi final against Leeds in 1970 is a record for a European competition game. Celtic's finest moment was without doubt the 1967 European Cup triumph in Lisbon, when the club became the first from Britain to win the trophy. An extraordinary feature of this success is that the club is the only one to win the trophy with a complete team of home-grown players - all eleven team members were born within thirty miles of Celtic Park.

KELVINGROVE PARK 1897 39757

Did You Know? GLASGOW
A MISCELLANY

QUIZ QUESTIONS

Answers on page 52.

1. In 1824 Charles Mackintosh invented the process of rubber-proofing cloth to make it waterproof, giving rise to the raincoat, or mackintosh. He was the son of a Highlander who operated a Dennistoun dyestuff factory - what steps were taken at this factory to prevent industrial espionage?

2. What is the generally accepted meaning of the name 'Glasgow'?

3. What are the names of the three rivers which flow through Glasgow?

4. Which long-running television series is located in Glasgow?

5. What and where is the oldest house in Glasgow?

6. By what name is St George's Place now known?

7. Where in Glasgow will you find a herd of Highland cattle?

8. Which Glasgow building was modelled on the Doge's Palace in Venice?

9. Glasgow has the world's only two-legged equestrian monument - where can you find it, and who does it commemorate?

10. Which Glasgow building is popularly known as the Armadillo?

ST VINCENT PLACE 1897 39764

Did You Know?
GLASGOW
A MISCELLANY

RECIPE

BLACK BUN

Black Bun has been popular in Scotland since the 18th century. It is often made for Christmas and Hogmanay, when it is served to First Footers with a glass of whisky. It is best baked 2-3 months before Christmas and stored, wrapped, in an airtight tin, to allow the flavour to mature.

Ingredients

For the pastry:
450g/1lb plain flour
¼ teaspoonful salt
225g/8oz butter

For the filling:
350g/12oz self-raising flour
1 teaspoonful cinnamon
1 teaspoonful ground ginger
¼ teaspoonful black pepper
450g/1lb seedless raisins
¼ teaspoonful ground nutmeg
450g/1lb currants
50g/2oz mixed peel (optional)
50g/2oz glacé cherries
100g/4oz blanched almonds, coarsely chopped
100g/4oz chopped walnuts
2 tablespoonfuls whisky
A small amount of milk
2 egg yolks, beaten

Did You Know?
GLASGOW
A MISCELLANY

Preheat the oven to 180 degrees C/350 degrees F/ Gas Mark 4. Mix the flour and salt together and rub in the butter until the mixture resembles fine breadcrumbs. Mix in 1 tablespoonful of cold water, and knead well to form a pastry dough. Grease either a loaf tin or a round cake tin. Set aside a piece of pastry for the lid, then roll out the remainder on a floured surface to about 5mm (¼ inch) thick. Line the loaf or cake tin with the pastry, moulding it against the sides and making sure there are no holes.

Mix all the dry ingredients for the filling together and stir well. Add the whisky and stir in, and then enough milk to bring it to a stiff consistency. Fill the tin with the mixture and smooth it off flat at the top. Roll out the pastry lid and lay it on loosely so that the cake mixture can rise a little. Push a long skewer through the lid and filling right to the bottom, in about 8 places. Lightly prick the lid all over with a fork, then brush the lid with the beaten egg yolks. Bake in the preheated oven for 2½-3 hours until done - test by inserting a skewer into the centre, which should come out clean when the bun is cooked through. Allow the bun to stand in the tin on a wire tray for about 30 minutes before turning out. Serve in slices.

Did You Know?
GLASGOW
A MISCELLANY

LANCEFIELD QUAY 2005 G11717

Did You Know?
GLASGOW
A MISCELLANY

RECIPE

CRANACHAN

This famous recipe is one of Scotland's most delicious desserts.

Ingredients

50g/2oz medium oatmeal
4 tablespoonfuls clear runny honey
3 tablespoonfuls whisky
300ml/10fl oz double cream
350g/12oz raspberries

Toast the oatmeal in a shallow layer on a sheet of foil under the grill for a few minutes, stirring occasionally, until it is evenly browned but not burnt. Leave to cool.

Whip the cream in a large bowl until soft peaks form, then gently fold in the oats, honey and whisky until well combined. Reserve a few raspberries for decoration, then layer the remainder with the oat mixture in four serving dishes. Cover and chill for two hours.

About 30 minutes before serving, transfer the glasses to room temperature. Decorate with the reserved raspberries and serve.

QUIZ ANSWERS

1. To prevent industrial espionage, all the staff at the factory had to be Gaelic-speaking.

2. 'The dear green place'.

3. The Clyde, the Kelvin and the Cart.

4. 'Taggart'.

5. Provand's Lordship in Castle Street, which was erected in 1471. It is now preserved as a museum.

6. Nelson Mandela Place.

7. Pollok Park.

8. The Templeton Carpet Factory in Templeton Street.

9. The statue is at the corner of Woodlands Road and Cliff Road. It commemorates the Scottish cartoonist Bud Neill, who trained at the Glasgow School of Art. The statue is of the cartoon character Lobey Dosser astride his horse El Fideldo (Elfie), and the cost of erecting the statue was met with the donations that were received following an appeal in the Glasgow Herald. The inscription reads: 'Statue erected by public subscription on May 1st 1992 to the memory of Bud Neill, 1911-1970, cartoonist & poet, creator of Lobey Dosser, Sheriff of Calton Creek, his sturdy steed El Fideldo, resident villain Rank Bajin, and many other characters.'

10. Glasgow's new Concert Hall at Finnieston, on the north bank of the Clyde (see photograph G11719, opposite).

Did You Know?
GLASGOW
A MISCELLANY

ATLANTIC QUAY 2005 G11718

THE CONCERT HALL 2005 G11719

FRANCIS FRITH

PIONEER VICTORIAN PHOTOGRAPHER

Francis Frith, founder of the world-famous photographic archive, was a complex and multi-talented man. A devout Quaker and a highly successful Victorian businessman, he was philosophical by nature and pioneering in outlook. By 1855 he had already established a wholesale grocery business in Liverpool, and sold it for the astonishing sum of £200,000, which is the equivalent today of over £15,000,000. Now in his thirties, and captivated by the new science of photography, Frith set out on a series of pioneering journeys up the Nile and to the Near East.

INTRIGUE AND EXPLORATION

He was the first photographer to venture beyond the sixth cataract of the Nile. Africa was still the mysterious 'Dark Continent', and Stanley and Livingstone's historic meeting was a decade into the future. The conditions for picture taking confound belief. He laboured for hours in his wicker dark-room in the sweltering heat of the desert, while the volatile chemicals fizzed dangerously in their trays. Back in London he exhibited his photographs and was 'rapturously cheered' by members of the Royal Society. His reputation as a photographer was made overnight.

VENTURE OF A LIFE-TIME

By the 1870s the railways had threaded their way across the country, and Bank Holidays and half-day Saturdays had been made obligatory by Act of Parliament. All of a sudden the working man and his family were able to enjoy days out, take holidays, and see a little more of the world.

With typical business acumen, Francis Frith foresaw that these new tourists would enjoy having souvenirs to commemorate their days out. For the next thirty years he travelled the country by train and by pony and trap, producing fine photographs of seaside resorts and beauty spots that were keenly bought by millions of Victorians. These prints were painstakingly pasted into family albums and pored over during the dark nights of winter, rekindling precious memories of summer excursions. Frith's studio was soon supplying retail shops all over the country, and by 1890 F Frith & Co had become the greatest specialist photographic publishing company in the world, with over 2,000 sales outlets, and pioneered the picture postcard.

FRANCIS FRITH'S LEGACY

Francis Frith had died in 1898 at his villa in Cannes, his great project still growing. By 1970 the archive he created contained over a third of a million pictures showing 7,000 British towns and villages.

Frith's legacy to us today is of immense significance and value, for the magnificent archive of evocative photographs he created provides a unique record of change in the cities, towns and villages throughout Britain over a century and more. Frith and his fellow studio photographers revisited locations many times down the years to update their views, compiling for us an enthralling and colourful pageant of British life and character.

We are fortunate that Frith was dedicated to recording the minutiae of everyday life. For it is this sheer wealth of visual data, the painstaking chronicle of changes in dress, transport, street layouts, buildings, housing and landscape that captivates us so much today, offering us a powerful link with the past and with the lives of our ancestors.

Computers have now made it possible for Frith's many thousands of images to be accessed almost instantly. The archive offers every one of us an opportunity to examine the places where we and our families have lived and worked down the years. Its images, depicting our shared past, are now bringing pleasure and enlightenment to millions around the world a century and more after his death.

For further information visit: www.francisfrith.com

INTERIOR DECORATION

Frith's photographs can be seen framed and as giant wall murals in thousands of pubs, restaurants, hotels, banks, retail stores and other public buildings throughout Britain. These provide interesting and attractive décor, generating strong local interest and acting as a powerful reminder of gentler days in our increasingly busy and frenetic world.

FRITH PRODUCTS

All Frith photographs are available as prints and posters in a variety of different sizes and styles. In the UK we also offer a range of other gift and stationery products illustrated with Frith photographs, although many of these are not available for delivery outside the UK – see our web site for more information on the products available for delivery in your country.

THE INTERNET

Over 100,000 photographs of Britain can be viewed and purchased on the Frith web site. The web site also includes memories and reminiscences contributed by our customers, who have personal knowledge of localities and of the people and properties depicted in Frith photographs. If you wish to learn more about a specific town or village you may find these reminiscences fascinating to browse. Why not add your own comments if you think they would be of interest to others? See **www.francisfrith.com**

PLEASE HELP US BRING FRITH'S PHOTOGRAPHS TO LIFE

Our authors do their best to recount the history of the places they write about. They give insights into how particular towns and villages developed, they describe the architecture of streets and buildings, and they discuss the lives of famous people who lived there. But however knowledgeable our authors are, the story they tell is necessarily incomplete.

Frith's photographs are so much more than plain historical documents. They are living proofs of the flow of human life down the generations. They show real people at real moments in history; and each of those people is the son or daughter of someone, the brother or sister, aunt or uncle, grandfather or grandmother of someone else. All of them lived, worked and played in the streets depicted in Frith's photographs.

We would be grateful if you would give us your insights into the places shown in our photographs: the streets and buildings, the shops, businesses and industries. Post your memories of life in those streets on the Frith website: what it was like growing up there, who ran the local shop and what shopping was like years ago; if your workplace is shown tell us about your working day and what the building is used for now. Read other visitors' memories and reconnect with your shared local history and heritage. With your help more and more Frith photographs can be brought to life, and vital memories preserved for posterity, and for the benefit of historians in the future.

Wherever possible, we will try to include some of your comments in future editions of our books. Moreover, if you spot errors in dates, titles or other facts, please let us know, because our archive records are not always completely accurate—they rely on 140 years of human endeavour and hand-compiled records. You can email us using the contact form on the website.

Thank you!

For further information, trade, or author enquiries
please contact us at the address below:

**The Francis Frith Collection, Unit 6, Oakley Business Park,
Wylye Road, Dinton, Wiltshire SP3 5EU.**

Tel: +44 (0)1722 716 376 Fax: +44 (0)1722 716 881
e-mail: sales@francisfrith.co.uk **www.francisfrith.com**